ABOUT THE AUTHOR

Thomasina Price was born in Birmingham and spent part of her childhood in Scotland. She loves dogs and has owned many, including some she has rescued. Thomasina enjoys reading history and local travel. She is currently working on a new book to include some of her past dogs.

GOODNIGHT, BUFFY

Loving a Lakeland Terrier

GOODNIGHT, BUFFY

Loving a Lakeland Terrier

Thomasina Price

A[...
or cr ...
Act ...
a ...
pul ...
the ...
conc ...

...
nts
in
h
es
ers.

Matador
9 Priory Business Park
Kibworth Beauchamp
Leicestershire LE8 0RX, UK
Tel: (+44) 116 279 2299
Fax: (+44) 116 279 2277
Email: books@troubador.co.uk
Web: www.troubador.co.uk/matador

ISBN 978 1780883 724

British Library Cataloguing in Publication Data.
A catalogue record for this book is available from the British Library.

Matador is an imprint of Troubador Publishing Ltd

Printed and bound in the UK by TJ International, Padstow, Cornwall

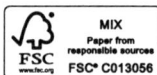

For my sister, Eileen, with love

CONTENTS

INTRODUCTION

This book began on Buffy's last weekend. As my time with Buffy was vanishing I felt a compulsion to write about her passing to ease my pain. I then felt the need to share Buffy's story and what made her such a special little dog, for hers wasn't just a story of doom and gloom.

Buffy was a Lakeland terrier. She was infuriating and inspiring, funny and cunning. I wanted to salute her bravery and thank her for showing me such happiness. She and I shared some dark times but she was always a beacon of hope and light for me. She even acquired her own fan club. I was astonished at how many people followed her treatment locally!

Buffy fought a long battle against cancer and

took the record for treatment time. We did go on to live happily ever after but with a few hiccups.

I have many memories of Buffy but the ones I share with you here are my favourites. And I know, even as the years pass, that when I read them she will be in front of me as vividly as ever she was in life. Perhaps after all, this is a love story.

ALL ABOUT BUFFY

Buffy was beautiful, like an overgrown Steiff teddy bear, all blue and tan curls. Every few months, however, come clip time the other Buffy emerged. Under the curls lay a square-jawed workmanlike terrier. She was a formidable and feisty girl; she never became a fawning or over-affectionate dog. The occasional pat or cuddle suited her. She was very much her own independent little person.

My sister Eileen fostered Buffy in 1997. As a two-year-old rescue dog, Buffy had arrived via a fellow park walker, a young girl who had found her hiding in a Blackpool shop doorway late one night in the driving rain. The girl traced the owners but they said they didn't want Buffy; she was a street dog, a hobo. The girl asked if she could have her and they gladly handed her over.

Buffy should have gone to live in her new home in Blackpool at this point but there was to be further tragedy. The young girl soon found out she had ovarian cancer and would need treatment in Birmingham, her old home. While there, she needed someone to foster Buffy and give her a permanent home. Eileen happily agreed.

Eileen was unsure whether she should adopt her, but I thought Buffy was an absolute gem and encouraged Eileen to keep her. A few months later the young girl died, at the age of twenty eight. Eileen attended the service at the ancient St Leonard's church in Frankley and took Buffy to wait for her in the car, in sight of the hearse of her old mistress.

A few weeks after Buffy arrived she was taken to the vets and spayed. The day after her discharge and on her first walk after surgery Buffy showed her true colours. Her head was barely visible behind the Elizabethan collar but it had given her an idea for a cracking plan. Poor Eileen! She never suspected that given

Buffy's condition she would be interested in catching a squirrel.

Buffy was off! She soon caught the squirrel and then bashed it into a tree trunk. Her final act, to everyone's horror, would be to use the tree trunk as a tool. Pushing her collar against the trunk Buffy managed to scoop and load the squirrel right into the collar. She then rushed straight back to Eileen to present her with the dead squirrel carefully draped inside her surgical collar.

The lesson was clear: all terriers can be ruthless but Buffy had raised the bar. Who would think a surgical collar could be used as a weapon and a tipper truck? Buffy was undoubtedly a genius in the worst possible way.

THE EARLY YEARS

Within a year I had joined Eileen's household as my health was failing and fairly soon it became apparent my condition was very serious. I was diagnosed with an incurable and progressively degenerative disease.

At this time our home was also shared with two lurchers, Emma and Liege, but for me, as unfair as it might be, Buffy was the shining star. Perhaps I knew we would share many battles and a treasure trove of happy times. In the coming years I would experience relapses and Buffy was there, giving me comfort with her presence as I lay paralysed, waiting for the time to pass and the movement to return to my body; it was always a long wait. Buffy was so often my reason to continue with the fight. So this is

Buffy's story and what a wonderful story it would turn out to be.

Four years passed with fun and contentment for Buffy. She spent sunny days in the garden with Emma and Liege, where all three dogs would rocket around, tracing out an imaginary racetrack. Buffy always wanted to be the fastest and last the longest. She couldn't outrun them, although she gave it a good try, but she could outlast them. She would go around on this ruddy racetrack for so long I worried she would get dizzy and keel over.

My, what fun we had on the way to the park with Buffy, Emma and Liege. I used to sing, "Roll me over in the clover" and the dogs all joined in, barking the chorus. I laughed and sang most of the way. They loved it. When we arrived at the park they shot out of the car and I felt complete happiness wash over me and a sudden and lovely peace! Of course this fun was nothing compared to the fun all three dogs had with Eileen. She was the main dog walker and took them up the Waseley hills and around vast reservoirs and all sorts of other delightful places.

EMMA AND LIEGE

It was always going to be hard for Buffy with Emma and Liege for truthfully they were very much "The Odd Couple" and Buffy would be playing gooseberry.

Liege or My Liege, to give his full title, was a stunning Saluki cross Whippet. A slender dog, he had an almost fawn-like brindle coat with a coal black mask. Once at midnight, while out walking with Eileen, he went off for a short while. This was quite out of character. Eileen caught sight of him in the distance. He was playing with a fox and they were both silhouetted by the moonlight. It was enchanting to watch as they played tag and boxed like mad March hares for a long time. At the end they gently sniffed each other and Liege wheeled round and returned to Eileen. Liege was a mystical creature and we felt this ethereal being must truly have belonged to an elvish queen.

Emma was originally a neighbour's dog and after meeting Liege a number of times she would escape her garden and run down the road to lie in Eileen's garden and wait all day if needs be, all the time barring her teeth to callers and ensuring the post would have to be collected from the sorting office! Shortly afterwards, Emma joined the household as her family could no longer keep her and with her safely inside normal postal deliveries resumed. Emma was a beauty, heavier set than Liege but with a coat that glowed like burnished gold on a summer's evening.

Emma and Liege were inseparable. Indeed, in their last years they walked the park paths together with their tails entwined. Liege had one of those long tails with a slight curl at the end; he used this hook-like tail end to grasp Emma's tail. It was quite a comical sight to walk behind and watch them toddle along like elephants in a circus. Emma and Liege had eyes for no one but each other but they recognised that Buffy was lonely and sometimes started a game for her. Emma was formidable in the park if any other dog tried to get rough with her. Emma appointed herself Buffy's guardian.

Buffy lost Emma and Liege within two months of 2002; it left her distraught. The day after Liege died Buffy sat on the sofa shaking violently. We reassured her for some time but ironically, although she was very upset, it left Buffy the only dog, which she soon came to love.

No more fighting to be top dog; there were no other dogs. Out of this lonely and very scared chrysalis a completely different dog would emerge, a very confident young dog who wanted to engage with the whole world and start making new friends.

NETWORKING

Ours was Buffy's third home that we knew of and she seemed to have reasoned that she must try very hard to be all things to all men.

Buffy was entered at an RSPCA fun day soon after joining our household, when she was looking her loveliest. When Eileen returned and showed me her haul of medals, I declared amazed, "What's with all the prizes?"

Buffy had swept the board and received nearly everything except the "Dog of the Show".

The organisers had whispered to Eileen, "We wanted to give her that as well but it wouldn't have been fair, she had won so much."

Buffy had struck again and charmed everyone.

Some years later on holiday in a remote part

of Scotland I walked Buffy past a fisherman's cottage, which had its front door very temptingly ajar. Buffy was some way ahead of me and I sensed she wouldn't be able to resist. Suddenly I heard a delighted cry asking if she had come for tea. The lady had turned around in her seat to see Buffy sitting sweetly next to the cake stand. Buffy then gave a little "Harrumph", her own peculiar noise. I had just reached the front door and started to apologise but the owner came out and said she was more than welcome to stay for tea: she would make a welcome companion.

Buffy was a great explorer and adventurer. Secret paths, woody woods and doors slightly ajar were there to be enjoyed and investigated and sometimes we met wonderful people or animals on these forays. It always helps explorers when they are social butterflies who can mingle!

Buffy liked getting back to her roots. One warm summer's day we visited the Waseley hills for a greyhound meet and benefit. It was going to take her some effort to shine and stand out at an event full of all these tall dogs! She decided to run up the hills and pick out a nice steamy, stinking cowpat. We watched in horror as she tore back down the hill to join us. We had to leave the meeting and drive home with eyes red from crying. We had tried cleaning her before the ride home and she had many vigorous baths after that but the stink stayed around for a few days. Buffy seemed delighted with a job well done.

ON STAGE

As the only dog in our household, Buffy's development seemed to notch up a gear. As Eileen and I were now her main companions and she was concentrating on us, her understanding of language and commands increased. Mostly self taught she could respond to many more words and, in her way, now tried to communicate with us.

No other dog quite made Buffy's noises. She had acquired a short funny "Harrumph" if she wanted your attention and also an "A-Wah". What was really endearing was something she started in her last five years: the "touch up". Buffy would get behind you and gently touch the back of your knee with her paw and then very tenderly run it down the length of your calf. Often, when I was in church or standing washing up, Buffy would softly touch me and take me by surprise.

Buffy's talking reminds me of trips to the library. After years of waiting patiently outside on visits, Buffy would summon me after about a minute. There would be a short woof followed by a cacophony of peculiar noises. Obviously all this chattering was a sort of "Hurry up missus" peeping out. I couldn't help but smile and say, "OK Buffy let's go."

And I would leave it for another day.

Our large bay window acted as Buffy's stage and I always smiled as I swung the car around to see her sitting there. Somehow with her natural beauty and chutzpah she reminded me of Marie Lloyd, the old vaudeville star. On this stage she could observe all, wait for callers, issue threats, sunbathe and play games! At night with the curtains closed she would intermittently shove her head through and give us a woof and I swear she was laughing. Oh Buffy, how we miss your curtain calls.

BOO TO YOU!

Walks became really fun after Buffy learned to "boo" and also demonstrated how smart a cookie she was. It first started when I hid behind a tree in Selly Oak Park after waiting for her to return to me. The young Buffy didn't care for the recall command; she had passed all her obedience tests but decided to forget them as soon as she left the training classes.

Buffy searched the park in an organised way, "Desperately searching for Thomasina". I jumped out from behind a tree and she was really mad! She had, however, learnt a new game, a game she would excel at. For a few months she would position herself behind a tree and surprise me with a sharp woof when I went past. It worked very well for a few times but when I got wise the game was abandoned.

But the bread delivery man at Shenley shops was not aware of Buffy or her new game. Every morning about 7am, I would go to the shops and tie Buffy outside to one of the pillars. On this morning the delivery man sauntered forward, happily balancing the bread-filled trays on his shoulders, his right arm balancing the load. With great stealth, Buffy waited for him behind the pillar. As he passed she jumped out with an almighty woof and sat back down.

I could hear the commotion from inside the shop. The delivery man had jumped so high the trays had all dropped and the loaves were scattered onto the floor. A regular customer outside the shop was doubled up with laughing.

"I saw her hiding; I tell you, he jumped so high he nearly left his shoes behind." I swear Buffy was laughing herself but, mission accomplished, she never played Boo again.

PAWROBICS!

Sarah Pickles rang the doorbell. Sarah was a rare species, a visiting physiotherapist. A lovely woman with a perfect cut-glass accent and perfect deportment. Her area covered south Birmingham and included Shenley. I was to start a short course of physiotherapy at home.

For Buffy this was a great networking opportunity; she loved making friends with new people. Buffy was also highly competitive, so exercise would be fun.

I remember I managed a few exercises without interruption. Buffy's beady eyes were fixed on me waiting for her chance to shine.

"Right, let's do some core exercises," said Sarah briskly.

I lay on my back and that's when Buffy joined

in. She lay on her back next to me on the rug, but she knew this was no tummy rub and, with perfect concentration, she stretched her back legs out further than ever before and looked briefly at me with a smug look. She was copying my movements and I have no doubt that she probably did find her core muscles. As I studied her I realised she was managing to pull her stomach back further than me. Typical Buffy!

From there it was on to using the stairs in the hall. I had to put one foot on the third stair and lean forward to stretch out my calf muscles on the opposite leg,

The thought went through my mind: "A-ha! That'll scupper Buffy's plans." But she knew how to top this. She ran up the stairs and sat down half way. Facing out towards Sarah she insisted on offering her paw to her through the open silver railings, making sure Sarah gave her attention to her.

At the end of the session Mrs. Pickles was enchanted and declared she planned to get a dog as soon as she retired. The dog, she decided, had to be a Lakeland terrier.

No doubt it was a survival tactic from her

early days but Buffy could be very charming and astute. She seemed to have a sixth sense on how to approach people. That approach might vary but she always behaved as an equal. She also managed to cross class barriers: she was appreciated by farmers or fine ladies and also, it seemed, physiotherapists!

BUFFY'S HEALTH BATTLES

The first of Buffy's battles happened when she was only three years old. Without warning, she couldn't walk; she just lay there in obvious, dreadful pain. At this time I could barely manage to walk myself. I remember it began when I took her a short walk to the shops. The trees were only about five feet apart on the way there and I tried to carry her but could hardly hold her. At each tree we would stop for maybe five minutes. I thought we would never make the short distance home.

The diagnosis was serious. She had a slipped disc and would need total cage rest for two weeks. But her condition couldn't be cured by cage rest – the only long-term cure was surgery. Somehow, we had to try and control her exuberance so the operation could be put back as far as possible.

In January 2003 we took Buffy to the vet because she had a limp. All over Christmas she had held her paw up and even tried running with it at a very odd angle. It didn't seem such a worry going to the vet. Perhaps it was a strain? X-rays showed the devastating truth: it was cancer. They would have to amputate her leg.

A further problem for us was that the biopsy did not confirm the type of cancer. Although the X-rays showed the growth all around her paw, the vet could not grab any cells to identify the type. The growth was entwined between her metatarsals like poison ivy and a delay could cost Buffy her life if it was shown to be a Fibro sarcoma, for they traveled like lightning to the chest. Also, the paw would drive her crazy; dogs have been known to chew off their legs to relieve the pain. Some manage to do this within a few hours.

Buffy was referred to a specialist the next day at the Willows Animal Hospital. Something told me that even given the perilous diagnosis it was something bad but not a Fibro sarcoma.

When the Willows couldn't identify the type after another biopsy and suggested amputation, we opted for Buffy to have a final referral to the world-famous Animal Health Trust near Newmarket.

Finally we had a definite result from a larger biopsy; Buffy had a Mixo sarcoma: a very rare but slower-growing cancer so we could at least try to fight to save her leg. It was obvious to us that Buffy could not manage on three legs as she was so vulnerable with her bad back. We had to save her leg to save Buffy.

The wait for the results on her final biopsy was excruciating. Little did we realise there would be many more painful waits for news during her treatment.

The fight to save Buffy's leg began in earnest in March 2003 after diagnosis. After an operation to remove as much as possible of the sarcoma Buffy required four weeks of radiotherapy at Cambridge University hospital to blast away at the sarcoma they couldn't remove. From there it should have been a few more visits just to check on the healing and then discharge. But Buffy was unlucky – the wound didn't heal. The vets tried many different options; every week we would pack up and return to the Animal Health Trust in Suffolk. Finally by the summer of 2004 the only option was for Buffy to have a skin graft from her side to close the open wound. Either that or leg amputation.

Buffy had the skin graft and then we were on tenterhooks to know if it had taken. It was the longest wait yet for us and so very tense. Each morning we waited for Buffy's surgeon Prue Neath to call. Prue was an angel and always called promptly at the start of her day, despite her huge workload.

Just as important to Buffy's treatment was the lovely Sue Murphy, who told us she had spent many weekends worrying and fretting about Buffy after she had finished the Radiotherapy. Sue had personally administered her treatment at this time, had done all her MRI scans and had been the vet who had triumphed with the biopsy.

The graft had been performed in three sections. The middle graft had taken and this covered 60% of the wound; the two outside sections failed. There would be a further wait to see if the healthy skin would grow to cover the areas that hadn't taken. The day came and we received the anticipated and dreaded call.

Good news: the graft now covered the whole wound. Finally the future looked bright for Buffy.

We had commuted to Suffolk over 40 times and driven many miles in the eighteen months of her treatment. The dedication and skill the vets gave Buffy was incredible, not just the operations they performed but various treatments and endless medical meetings. Most remarkable of all was the international cooperation, for Buffy was sent a copper regeneration cream on special license from the United States of America. The cream was originally used for the victims of the Oklahoma bombings and Buffy would be the first dog to use it. In fact, the Animal Health Trust had thrown everything at her to help save her leg! Buffy would hold the record for vet visits and recovery time at the end of her treatment.

Even during her treatment Buffy's indomitable spirit shone through. Prue Neath soon found out about her scheming. Each morning Prue went about doing her ward rounds, checking her patients for progress. Buffy soon made her feelings clear: no other dog could be attended to before her or there would be bedlam. Buffy would throw herself about her cage barking and making clear her displeasure. Prue said she made it impossible for her to do her work changing dressings and doing all the other checks. All the nurses loved Buffy for she was such a character.

Nothing could cure her of this so, for peace, Buffy was always attended to first and then she was taken off the ward and out for a walk. After all this performance Buffy reverted to behaving impeccably. She was in hospital for many weeks and gained a following and fan club incorporating all the staff.

Truly they must be saints at the Animal Health Trust, not just for their world- renowned excellence but also for their patience! At one time Buffy had even worked out a way to turn her collar around – in fact, to turn it inside out – by using the cage bar wires. Forewarned about this, the vets made her an extra-long and reinforced collar. Perhaps she had belonged to Houdini in a former life.

During all this time of commuting and treatment, including quite a number of weeks of her staying over, Buffy had always jumped up and watched the packing of the car with enthusiasm. It was because of this we carried on. On the day of our final visit we were ecstatic it was over. A few days later we packed and traveled to Scotland and we were overjoyed to see her racing down a motel corridor with her Pudsey bear toy as always carried in her mouth.

Still there would be one further visit to the Animal Health Trust. As we had dreaded, the slipped disc problem re-emerged with a vengeance eighteen months later. This time bed rest wouldn't help; for a few months in 2005 her back was niggling away at her and then one dark night it almost killed her.

Buffy lay on her side in the most terrible pain, her chest moving up and down like bellows. She needed an emergency visit to the local vet and a dose of morphine. The verdict came next day: euthanasia or immediate surgery. Once again we elected for surgery. This time the neurology team at the Animal Health trust galloped to the rescue. The surgery was very risky but the recovery time was swift compared to the treatment time for the tumour. Buffy was operated on and home within a month and that included recovery time at hospital. The surgery success was aided by our taking her swimming and giving her physiotherapy.

The constant journeys for her main surgery for the sarcoma would test me both financially and physically. Eileen found it hard, too, because she did all the driving. Usually we visited the vet every week; most months we clocked up over a thousand miles.

In all we had traveled over 10,000 miles and Buffy would take the record for her treatment time. The struggle was worth it, though, for she enjoyed many more years.

Also, in saving Buffy I saved myself. I became a better person, more understanding and more interested in other people. My priorities in life had changed. I had been blessed.

THE DROWSY PARROT

After the initial diagnosis at The Oaks we decided to try alternative medicine as well as the conventional. We all trooped off to the craft centre at Earlswood Lakes because we had heard of a good crystal shop there. We didn't seriously think any of these alternative strategies would cure her but it kept us busy, gave us hope and gave Buffy a day out.

At Earlswood Lakes Buffy left sporting a small pale blue crystal on her collar; I can't say I remember its name or qualities. The shopkeeper thought this crystal most useful for her condition. Buffy soon lost it but we did come away with a recommendation for an expert in animal Reiki.

Some days later we visited the Reiki master

in a quiet road in leafy and rural Cheswick Green. A really lovely "new age" home with a very lively and noisy parrot. After we explained Buffy's predicament, the man started working on her, laying her on her side and touching her. It was remarkable how quickly she responded. Since the onset of the sarcoma she had been very fractious and unsettled, but for now she seemed to be at peace. The treatment lasted for nearly an hour but I had noticed other changes. I felt drowsy and rather detached, the air hung heavy and still and it was so very quiet there seemed to be an almost hypnotic silence.

I looked up and realised the parrot had started to list heavily to portside, was he hypnotised or had he fallen asleep? Quite alarmed I asked the "Master" about this.

"He's sleeping," he replied.

I had no idea how parrots slept but I suppose they wouldn't lie down with a pillow. For me the session had lost its tranquility. I had come to help my dog's leg and I was now transfixed by the parrot. Holding my breath I just hoped it wouldn't fall off and break its spindly leg!

Suddenly I felt we were acting in some farce.

I kept picturing Margaret Rutherford in "Blithe Spirit" and the scene with the séances with the parrot. We told the "Master" we would be in touch to let him know what had happened to Buffy. I wanted to call him many times to say, "Buffy is ok, she made it." Superstition stopped me.

I felt it would be tempting providence to call and say that she had been cured. So thank you, "Master". Incidentally, Buffy was a much happier dog after her visit.

WEST BAY

For over five years we would make many prolonged visits to West Bay. Our brother-in-law was very ill and died in the January of 2005 and we wanted to help support Anna, our sister, and keep her company. Since then it has almost become a second home.

West Bay seemed to be a magical place for Buffy. She loved the harbours, the seaside and the boats. I would take her at all times of day and night to enjoy it; it is such a stunning place. It is a very small town that has grown around a beautiful natural harbour. On the east side lies the sweeping cliffs and a treacherous coastal path that leads to Burton Bradstock. To the west, Anna's home stands on West cliff, which leads to National Trust land and exquisite Eype with the wonderful church looking out to sea and over to Portland Bill and the Jurassic coast.

Buffy wanted to explore everywhere; we wandered past the harbourmaster's house and down the ancient covered alley that led to George Street, following in the footsteps of many an ancient mariner. Down George Street stood "Olya's" shop. Olya had made a fuss of Buffy once and Buffy had never forgotten. Perhaps she had been enchanted by Olya's accent but no matter what time we passed, Buffy would run to the door and softly tap on it with her paw. Then back around to the harbour to watch the view of the boats being worked on and to sniff the shingle behind all the dry docks and fishermen's cottages.

When we had finished exploring and it was time to go home we would pass the lovely whitewashed St Johns Church, the old fishermen's church facing the harbour. I had taken Buffy here just once and I had prayed for my brother-in-law. This had been his church and his service had been held here after his death.

It came as a surprise when Buffy first sat

outside the church; I had no intention of entering it that day. I opened the door and Buffy shot in and sat at the pew behind the brass plaque with Wallace's name on. We never missed the church after that. Buffy always sat at the door and if it was open we went in and she always walked into the same pew and sat behind the plaque. At times she seemed to be as mystical as a unicorn.

In the evenings we would sit on a bench looking out to sea and sometimes we shared a crab sandwich at the George Inn. It's a privilege to spend time in this part of Dorset even in the enveloping cold of winter with a biting wind coming in off the sea and driving down the beautiful Jurassic coast. With the sea mists and the ever-changing sky it is staggeringly beautiful and to share it with Buffy, well, it was the icing on the cake.

LADIES WHO LUNCH
AND GO RATTING

Buffy was always a pleasure to take out and about, she networked as well as any career girl and always behaved impeccably if she was with people outside. She would politely introduce herself by sidling up to them and giving a gentle woof if they had taken her interest. Buffy always basked in admiration.

A favourite place to pose and watch the world go by was the bakery at Bournville Green. Eileen would meet up with us for lunch and we would enjoy some little pastries with tea and chat for an hour. After this I would take Buffy over to the small park across the road. Passing people would always smile and laugh for she had to walk on the high wall that separated the green from the pavement. Probably she had seen the children from Bournville school doing it and she decided to copy them. She looked very amusing.

Once we got to the park and Buffy was off the lead the other side to her nature materialised. I don't know if anything had ever lived under the bowling shed but Buffy had no doubts something had been there or was still using it. She was on a mission and I had to wait for ages while she inched around the perimeter, sniffing the irresistible odour drawing her there. I recognised the behaviour from many years before when she would go up and down the canals at Wolverhampton, relentlessly looking for rats. You can take a terrier from Lakeland but the drive and the determination stays.

OH SO PRETTY,
OH SO CHARMING IS SHE

A mile outside Belbroughton, down a narrow lane with high hedgerows lies Drayton and the Robin Hood Inn. A lunch time stop here with Buffy was the scene of one of her great conquests: "Bentley Boy."

On this day I was distinctly poorly with toothache and thought coming out would take my mind of the dull aching pain. I'd noticed a man draw up in the car park, a middle aged man, pleasant looking, driving a beautiful Bentley convertible. The man parked and walked over to join a group of his friends seated near to us.

Usually Buffy was well behaved but not today. After a few minutes she became fidgety.

First came the paw, then she gently teased a paw down my calf. Next we had the funny "Harrumph" and "A-Wah"; her demands were now persistent.

I became aware of eyes watching us intently. Transfixed by Buffy, "Bentley Boy" called over. "She wants you to speak to her"

I answered, "Yes I know."

To appease him and Buffy I reached down and gave her a quick tickle behind the ear and tried to carry on chatting.

Buffy wanted more attention and this time her "Harrumphs" and touching up increased tenfold. In pain and desperation I told her a rhyme we used and played with her a little imaginary tug of war.

"I'm a hip hop tip top Lakeland puppy,
My handle is Scruffy Buffy."

Looking up I noticed "Bentley Boy" was quite besotted by her and was totally mesmerised. Buffy could charm most men and bizarrely they were often the macho or affluent. I wished I could have held someone's attention for that long!

Again one day going around Bournville

Lake, on a day a local model boat regatta was taking place and the grounds were packed, Buffy had vanished. "Where could she be?"

She didn't usually vanish when there was nothing to take her interest so I was getting worried. Then a head popped out of the clubhouse – "The Bournville Model Yacht and Powerboat Club" no less.

Had she secured membership? Lucky Buffy!

"It's okay, we've been feeding her sausage rolls."

Buffy strolled casually out to the admiring glances of her model boat fan club. The door was then firmly shut behind her as it's a very private place, you know. Buffy, my Bournville star!

CAR CRAZY

We may have been responsible for this behavioural trait in Buffy: I devised some truck spotting to pass the time travelling, and perhaps this subconsciously affected her. We decided our targets were to be the Knights of Old lorries. You can't miss these wonderful pale blue lorries in central and eastern England. It was fun to look out for them. Emblazoned on the side of a Knight's lorry is a life-size Knight in shining armour, mounted on a fine charger and tilting his lance. Well, it gave us a lot of fun counting them, each sighting raising a loud cheer!

That wasn't the only time Buffy showed her love of travel and a keen interest in cars. I once called out Green flag for my car at home when I needed some assistance. I'm sure Buffy had noticed on the motorway that lorry drivers often had their dogs as driving mates in their cab and was secretly envious. Anyway, she had obviously watched the arrival of the large pick-up outside our house with longing. I was about to go with the man to get a part for my car but Buffy was bereft.

"I think she wants to get in your car," I joked.

"Okay," he replied, "I'll take her for a drive."

Bless him, as he wasn't busy he took us both for a drive. So off we traveled down nearby leafy lanes for a good fifteen minutes. It was all too much for Buffy, sitting on high looking out and being right next to the driver on a bench seat; all day she was on cloud nine and quite dreamy.

Almost as good, I had acquired the use of a mobility scooter because a friend of Eileen's had got a new one for his father, Fred, who had been a Bevin Boy in the war. I felt a bit of a fraud charging about on Fred's scooter, even though only in the hot weather, as I'm not anywhere near as disabled as he was, but it certainly helped with taking Buffy out occasionally. I can't say Buffy loved it at first, she wanted to walk as long as possible. But I persevered and lifted her up when she was tired and once she got the hang of it, she was made up!

One day, while sitting in my lap on the scooter, Buffy saw a large dog and was converted; neck stretched and head held high, she sat in my lap like Boudeacia in her chariot. For Buffy thought she was going into battle. Every time we whizzed past a large dog such as a Rottweiler she would give them a "Harrumph" and viewed them imperiously from on high. She loved her useful tools, especially when they restored her alpha status.

GOLDEN YEARS

The years rolled by. As is inevitable, Buffy became slightly arthritic and sometimes a little incontinent! Routine tests at the vet confirmed that, like many older dogs, Buffy's kidneys were failing. This meant after immediate admittance to have her kidneys flushed, she would need a special diet for the rest of her life. She would also need regular injections and would get Vit B and Cartofen monthly; and every 6 weeks a steroid called Laurobolin. She would also be monitored for rising levels of Creatine and Urea to make sure they were within acceptable margins.

That aside, life would go on as normal for Buffy but she was slowing down considerably. She still took incredible pleasure coming out for coffee with me and seeing people watching her. She never lost her delight at charming new people and being in new places, from the local church to the beautiful Victorian conservatory in Kings Heath Park. Nearly everyone smiles at a Lakeland.

Buffy had now acquired a new nickname: "Leaky Linda" and she could still muster an attack on the red vacuum cleaner she so disliked. In her golden years each attack on the Hoover would be followed by her leaking a few spots on the carpet, which I quietly cleaned up with a little tissue. It didn't matter. Eileen and I knew she was on limited time and she was still having some fun!

In the early years of her illness (Buffy lived with her failing kidneys for two years) she still tried to follow me around. If I was upstairs on the computer she would come up the stairs and do that silly talk of hers. I would laugh and say, "OK then, Buffy, let's go out." And I would take her for a drive and maybe a coffee in Bromsgrove.

As she grew older, Buffy's pursuits were of a gentler persuasion; dogs are really like people with the passing years – we all like to stop and sniff the flowers. Buffy would stop and raise her head and drink deeply of nearly every flower's fragrance, as dedicated as any bee to her task. After this came the crushing phase. I didn't have the heart to stop her every time but she would throw herself over the banks of daffodils and roll over. Nothing could match her pleasure at rolling amongst clouds of yellow daffodils!

Back at home and with the ever-lengthening naps, Buffy took up burping. Dear old Emma had taken up farting as her recreational sport; Buffy missed out on that and instead enjoyed burping. In her last year she would stretch out against my leg on the sofa and I would gently stroke her until she burped ever so softly. The stroking couldn't stop until Buffy was burped and all the time she looked at me blissfully.

One of my favourite photographs of Buffy was taken in her later years. She was snapped on the Severn Valley Railway one September twilight time. We had traveled from Kidderminster to Bridgnorth and had spent most of the day slowly walking and admiring assorted views, then making our way home. Buffy sat on the dining table of the train between our facing seats and looked so happy and content. She amused so many people, particularly a couple in a train pulled alongside. The two trains were standing together waiting for some time (probably a points change). The couple laughed and said hello to her and she looked up and stretched her head to acknowledge them and received a cheer. How regal she could be!

FADING AWAY

The years mellowed Buffy. I have no doubt she had some reasoning of how ill she had been and how her days had shortened, and her personality changed considerably. The humour was still there but kindliness came to her. She gave up barking at cats and even tolerated an old tabby stray moving in. She did draw the line at making friends with him though, and rejected all his sweet advances!

At this time Eileen was nursing a friend with a failing liver and Buffy always accompanied her on her visits. Buffy had no doubts she was another carer. For over a year, three times a week, Buffy would look forward to visiting Christine and quietly sitting by her feet, listening to her and passing the evening; a small friendly and ailing group with a shared camaraderie.

An incident towards the end of her life really stunned me and I realised how astute Buffy could be. I am hopeless with keys and every morning before we left the house, I would be calling out loudly, "Where are my keys?"

On this day Buffy sighed and lightly woofed, then started digging deeply between the sofa seats with only her bum sticking out to show she was there. She reappeared, having fished out my house keys and brought them over to me. She then sat at my feet and voiced her little "Harrumph", followed by a sigh. Buffy never brought me things! She didn't care one jot for retrieving.

I knew then that Buffy had known all along where I had lost my keys and had probably known every morning where I'd lost them. All these years she had enjoyed watching the show.

Soon Buffy could no longer climb the stairs and if I had to go upstairs she would wait for me as near as she could make it to the foot of the stairs. After that she was happy to follow me downstairs and then when even that was too tiring she lay in the corner of the sofa and often dozed. Her devotion was constant and even now I can see her beautiful dark eyes looking intently at me. She seemed to be all wise. Buffy, I miss you so.

The last winter I spent mostly in her company downstairs. My mind flew back to all the times she lay next to me during my illness and her presence kept my hopes up. Then again, I remembered the times when she was recuperating from her treatment at the Animal Health Trust and I would lie besides her on the bed and sing Greensleeves to her.

Strangely, after her recovery she would move away if she heard that tune. I am told that dogs do not have associations but I swear Buffy could not tolerate that song and recognised it if it was playing on the television or the radio.

We spent our time together with me reading or just quietly reflecting, two dear chums together, waiting for the inevitable and making sure that every minute counted.

BUFFY'S PASSING

Friday 20th February 2010

An appointment has been made for Buffy at 5.10 this afternoon. The last few days she hasn't eaten or been her usual self so Eileen and I take her to the vet. Straight away, Kieron tells us she is very dehydrated, she has also lost weight for the 3rd month. She's to be kept in overnight, put on a drip to give her some fluids and will have more tests on her kidneys.

Saturday 21st February 2010

Kieron calls before 10 am and the news is awful. Buffy's kidneys are worse and she has no more than two weeks to live. We go to the vet and Kieron explains Buffy's kidneys are no longer just failing, they are malfunctioning; this means they are poisoning her. I know it is the end when Kieron tells me the readings for her tests. Kieron adds there is nothing more he can do to save her. Another flush of her kidneys will not really help. She now has two weeks to live and it won't be a pleasant end. This would be a dreadful end if we were to leave it to its own course. She cannot eat – it will make her sick – so it would be a long, slow, agonising end without euthanasia. Buffy is facing a terrible storm in her life and it is in our hands to keep her safe and at peace. Buffy will be euthanased before the full force of this storm hits her.

We have decided to take Buffy home for now. She will have a strong injection to last her over the weekend. This weekend will be Buffy's last and she will spend it doing what Buffy likes to do. On Monday at 1pm Buffy will be put to sleep.

We stop off at Bournville on the way to Cath's and get the gang some turkey. Cath's a good friend and has many dogs. Buffy always enjoys visiting here. It's lots of fun for her with the jostling and asserting herself as top dog. It is too much to bear, knowing we only have two days with her and it is tearing us apart watching her playing with the others. We know she has a very short time to feel okay, so we stay for an hour only. Remarkably, she eats a little turkey and leaves not too tired.

At home Buffy sleeps in her usual spot on the sofa and is not too fussed about going out. The most important thing is that she's drinking a little water but she wants no more food.

Buffy and Tess have been together a long time. In 2002 I returned to work for a short time and Buffy and Tess were both day boarders with Cath – or school as we jokingly called it. It wasn't for too long but since then Tess has spent time here at home with Buffy. Every week Tess stays with us for a few days and she will miss her.

Heavy snowfall doesn't help for it makes it dangerous to walk Buffy in this area. I hate this winter. It is the hardest in 30 years and I can hardly get out. How I'd love a nice fine day for Buffy and me.

We keep stroking and loving Buffy and for the next two nights we will both sleep with her. It is unbearable watching the hours and minutes ticking away and counting down her remaining time. Kieron has told us letting Buffy go is the last thing we can do for her but the heartache and feelings of desolation are overwhelming. I feel physically sick and dizzy and walk around like a zombie. How will we ever get through this? We keep talking about Buffy and to her, for although she is tired sometimes she looks up and is listening and watching us. The mental strain is unbearable and I feel close to collapse. "I love you so much, Buffy."

This first night of sleeping with Buffy is more of an ordeal for me than her. I cannot sleep as I lie beside her. I must keep looking at her to commit every little thing of her to memory. Buffy is heart breakingly sweet, with the softest and shallowest breaths; she sleeps soundly. So I decide to lie at the bottom of the bed on the floor so as not to rouse her. I feel dreadful, my emotions in a whirlpool.

Sunday 21st February 2010

We wake up to fresh snow on the ground and give an inward groan. We have got up early so Buffy can have one last walk around her favourite place, Selly Oak park, and have one last trip with all the other dogs. Putting on her little navy coat it upsets me to see how much weight she has lost from around her tummy. I am anxious when Eileen tries to drive off, the wheels spin and the car won't go forward. Eileen turns the car and goes in the other direction.

After the walk everyone comes back together to the car park. Buffy hangs back as Cath loads the gang into her car. Cath picks up Buffy and, softly crying and kissing her, she returns her to Eileen.

Buffy comes home. She has taken some treats from Cath and has enjoyed her walk. It has been a gentle walk just sniffing and strolling together for all the four-legged fellowship. It is the last time Buffy will be one of the SODS (Selly Oak Dog Squad) in this realm.

In the afternoon I take Buffy to Bournville

Park. She likes it here; it is nice and flat and has a lovely stream flowing through. I let her stroll and take her time. I pick some crocuses to press for memories' sake. In the last few months although she hasn't until now had a bad patch, I have said to her, "Buffy please stay until the snowdrops come."

Monday 22nd February 2010

Today will be Buffy's last day. Last night was just another night like the one before. How will we bear it today? But we know it is right for we notice that the injection Kieron gave for the weekend is only just holding her together. Buffy doesn't see to be in pain but has no energy at all. After an hour, a slight break, she wants to go down the road to Spiceland Green. Nothing to do after this except await Kieran's visit. Buffy is due to be put to sleep at 1pm but just before then we take a call to say it will be around 4.30pm; Kieron is held up in theatre.

The wait is the most trying of experiences. Buffy was sick at one point, just fluids. At 3pm I say to Eileen, "I can't just wait for her to die – right now she's alive."

How wonderful, Buffy manages a little stroll! We have come to the green opposite the house and my little sweetheart eats some snow, as always, and has a roll (of sorts) – she manages to rub her head and shoulder in the snow.

The moment we have been dreading arrives. Kieron and a nurse come to our house. Kieron explains that he has left the little shunt in from Buffy's last visit and will give her a small tranquilliser to start. This will make her drowsy and then the final injection, which will stop her heart. With the tranquilliser we have a final chance to say goodbye to Buffy and tell her we love her.

She is sleeping in the corner of the sofa. I sit on the floor at her side and Eileen is next to her. We both say how much we love her and what a good dog she is and kiss her on the head. Aware that hearing is the last thing to go, I tell her she will be going to the park. We do not cry. We do not want Buffy to pass over hearing us cry and be frightened or upset.

The final injection and Kieron tells us that her heart has stopped. It is then that the floodgates open. We thank Kieron and the nurse and they quickly leave.

I throw my head back and scream. I can't stop it. Eileen takes Buffy upstairs and lays her gently on her bed which she has always shared with Eileen, and for the next two days and nights, until we can take her to the crematorium for her allotted slot, we will keep Buffy up here. For once the cold weather is in our favour. The heating is turned off and windows opened to keep the house cold.

I will sleep with Buffy Monday night and Eileen will take Tuesday. We both keep going into the room to look at her and think about the young dog that came into our lives and shared it for over twelve years.

I gently cut the pink bandage on her leg slightly apart; Buffy would have hated it. Then I see the shunt in her leg. There must have been quite a few times Buffy had a splint in her leg and it brought it home to me what a brave little dog she had been.

We look in on her constantly and first I and

then Eileen pass the night sleeping with her with an arm gently touching her. One of her eyes is open a tiny bit and to see it without that powerhouse of life behind it. Well, it is so hard to comprehend.

Wednesday 24th February 2010

The very last day in this final goodbye has come. We have picked this crematorium because we can take Buffy and wait for her and bring her ashes home. The cremation is booked for 9.30am and we leave at eight. It may be too early to start out but we can sit a while and compose ourselves. The traffic to Stourbridge is light and the final road is just a farm track past many fields full of horses and it seems very calm and peaceful.

We wait outside the crematorium; it's now a quarter to nine. Buffy is on my lap. We sit mostly in silence. Eileen reaches over to touch her occasionally and I just want to study every feature of her and commit them to memory. Buffy is so beautiful there is nothing scary about her. In fact, the bad breath you associate with kidney failure is gone; she is just a very pretty sleeping girl.

At exactly 9.30am the owner of the crematorium comes to the car and gently lifts Buffy off me and takes her in. The waiting room is almost like a small prayer room. We sit around a large, dark wooden table and have to view caskets and consider if we would like an epitaph in the remembrance book and a brass plaque on her casket. Now the owner invites us to look at her a last time. Buffy has been placed in the most beautiful wooden basket.

We are told to say our goodbyes now. We do say goodbye and we also read out psalm 23 from the old family bible and then Eileen says we will take her in and be with her to the last minute. Buffy cannot go into the dark on her own, she might be frightened. After she is put in and the crematorium door is open we pat her and tell her we love her and we will see her some day soon. We retire to the waiting room until the procedure is finished. We pass the time mostly in silence with the occasional reminiscence about Buffy.

Coming home is the saddest journey after this, almost as unbearable as Mama's funeral and passing. A notice in the chapel catches my eye.

"The price of love is the pain of separation."

We place an epitaph in the memorial book at Prestwood for Buffy:

Buffy Price, A Lovely Lakeland
We have always loved you and we always will

Thursday 25ᵗʰ February 2010

There have been so many texts talking of Buffy, and a lovely condolence card from Margaret. I also write two letters to talk about Buffy, a thank you letter to her vets and the Animal Health Trust and a eulogy to Buffy. In the lavender border by the front door a snowdrop has appeared; we have never seen snowdrops anywhere in the garden and have never planted any. Perhaps snowdrops stay dormant but what a strange moment for it to show.

Letter to Sue Murphy at AHT

Dear Sue
Very sad news: we said a final farewell to our beloved

Buffy yesterday. Our vet kindly put her to sleep at home. We are inconsolable. She was unique, a tenacious, funny, loyal little girl. No other dog could replace her.

We would like to say a final thank you to you, Sue. Perhaps you could do us one last favour. We often wonder if Buffy still holds the record for treatment time (some 20 months commuting), and were any lessons learnt from her recovery?

We would love to hear from you about this.
Thomasina and Eileen Price

Letter to Kieron Corry, Buffy's vet

To Kieron & all staff at Manor Vets

Thank you all for your kindness shown towards Buffy. By visiting her at home you made her passing peaceful.

Buffy is irreplaceable. As a younger dog she roared through life, fearless and funny. Later she took the same approach to her treatment at the AHT for cancer.

Traveling to the AHT we stopped at some woods nearby to let her out. To our horror there was a 4x4 off-road course next door. She slipped in there wearing her Elizabethan collar and bandages and went up and down impossible gradients, covered the course and came back laughing.

Buffy was also very steadfast and loving in times of trouble.

All dogs are special but Buffy was sprinkled with stardust.

Thomasina and Eileen Price

Saturday 27th February 2010

Cath has left a beautiful plant at our door, an Escollonia; it will make a tall white evergreen shrub. I am very touched but later on looking at it closely I find a silver tag saying "Sweet Gentle Buffy" and on the reverse it says "I will always miss you". I cannot stop my tears; this is a real physical pain I am feeling.

Wednesday 3rd March 2010

I wake up, having dreamt of Buffy. I was at a large old-fashioned railway station in London. Suddenly I am aware I have Buffy with me and we must make the train for I am taking her on a journey. I can see people filing on the train at the front, I call but they cannot hear me. The train pulls out but suddenly stops for us. Running down the platform I pause at a guard's office, I see our family bible, the same one we took to Buffy's cremation. I take it down from on top of a pile of books – Buffy will need this for her journey – and then we reach the train. The only way on to this train is at the front and, as I can't climb up to the stairs, I must be lifted up by an iron ledge on the front of the train that can be raised. I grip Buffy tightly; she must not be scared for this is the train to the afterlife.

Thursday 4th March 2010

Although I don't attend the church services I have spent many hours in the past with Buffy at St David's church coffee mornings. We have whiled away the time, me drinking coffee and us sharing biscuits followed by lighting a candle and sometimes Buffy has received healing from Nick the vicar. I think it is important to visit and tell people of her passing and thank Nick.

I am hugged a number of times and then

when I ask Nick if he might bless her ashes he takes me into the Healing room. Buffy has her own little service performed with two others. We all pray for Buffy and she is brought to God's attention. Later that afternoon we have returned home after a trip to Staffordshire, a card says some flowers have been delivered for us next door. Astonishingly, a beautiful bouquet with daisies, chrysanthemums and Lilies has arrived from Kieron and Manor Vets. It seems Buffy touched many people.

Monday 8th March 2010

Awake after another night dreaming of Buffy. Opposite the bed there is a photograph of her but it was not this picture. In my dream I looked at a modern, large gilt-edged photo frame, the picture within it changed constantly and every picture was another memory of Buffy, another place and another time with her in the past. It was as if I was taking a whirlwind tour of her life. Oh precious, must I really only see you in dreams now. I miss you so.

The following days.

It is just as hard now, the living without Buffy, for she has been with me constantly for so many years. I miss so much about her, from the moment when her soft footfall going down the stairs is no longer audible, to the last moment when I say, "Goodnight, Buffy, it's bedtime."

The hours in between are impossible to fill without her. We would go everywhere together: the shops, visiting, walking or just sitting together on the sofa or having a nap when either of us was tired. There are times when it doesn't register Buffy is gone, it's if she's having one of her prolonged stays at the Animal Health Trust many years ago and soon her two or three weeks will be up and we will be going to collect her.

Another time I reach into the hall cupboard and put my hand on her blanket. I hold her blanket close to me and just bury my head in it and sob and just thinking of it now reduces me to tears. Oh my sweet precious, I didn't realise my love was so overwhelming.

Time is precious, especially when you are unsure when it will be taken from you. For

Buffy travelled to many wonderful places: heaths, canals, deserted beaches, woods and many events and now when I look back, gosh I had the best ten years of my life. So here's to Buffy, my brave and funny little girl.

"Goodnight Sweetheart."

POSTSCRIPT

June 2010

It has been just over three months since Buffy's passing. It is remarkable how, even in recent days, people I don't know stop and ask after her.

Three months on and some mornings I open her doggy travelling bag just to smell her pungent biscuits. On opening a drawer and finding Buffy's vet's purse, my heart skips a beat then starts racing.

In the hall we have a headshot of Buffy on the bookshelf next to her lead. I try to touch it but it's as if there is a forcefield around it. I can feel her energy buzzing out of it and even now my hand just trembles inches away from it.

Inside me I can feel a humming that is almost radioactive. I cannot recall ever having this reaction with grief before.

ACCEPTANCE

I found it hard moving forward, I never expected this emotional battering. I knew it wasn't that I was getting older and facing questions about my own mortality. I wanted to know more about Buffy and her place in the world; I couldn't believe – and still don't – that she was just another dog.

Buffy was one of many dogs I have owned over the years and I believe all pets are sentient creatures capable of complex emotions. Buffy, however, seemed so much more. She seemed to have crossed to another and higher level of being and she had transcended into a real person within a small doggy body. I have never met a creature so astute and wise, with real intelligence, using both intuition and calculation.

Buffy was very much "her own person".

I found myself reading a lot about dogs and all animals. I found comfort in the words of Mahatma Gandhi and Abraham Lincoln, both believers of basic animal rights. Most of all, I found myself wondering about Buddhist beliefs and reincarnation. I still have no answers. Who knows – certainly not me – but looking back, I had felt since Buffy had finished her treatment for her slipped disc in 2005 that there might be something more.

In the last years with Buffy, and with the passing of time being uppermost in my mind, I tried really hard to show how very loved she was. On the evenings when I had to leave for work I kissed her gently on the forehead and as the nights closed in and I felt her slipping away I would add I loved her very much and what a good girl she was. Her eyes followed me out of the door and I know she listened to me turning over the car engine. On walks on high lands and viewing points I held her up to see the view. Buffy always reminded me of Kate Winslett on the brow of the Titanic for she looked intently at the whole panorama in front of her. I lifted her up at so many places: Hardy's point in Dorset, the wild cliffs on the Moray Forth and at Frankley Beeches amongst many. Always, when her best doggy pal Tess stayed over for a few days, I would fling open the door and although Buffy was the last one in, being older, she was always the one I welcomed first with outstretched arms.

I think we had achieved unparalled closeness since both our illnesses were shared and reinforced our companionship. It never leaves me, the image of Buffy returning one evening from Eileen's friends, Terry and Jackie, in the most terrible temper. I heard Eileen and Buffy pull up on the drive and no sooner had Eileen put the key in the lock than Buffy hurled herself at the living room door and came screaming towards me. She had never done this before but I just knew she had asked for something out of their fridge and was refused. I was right.

I miss Buffy's soft footfall as she came down the stairs in the morning, her deep dark nose touching me and the endless curls my fingers stroked and became entwined with. Oh my sweetheart how soft and lovely you were.

I have many flowers collected on our walks, pressed into many books and secret places. In the last years I collected them to remind me of our many walks in the country and often a book will hold forget-me-nots from a riverbank or tiny pink or red wayside flowers from many far away trips. From Buffy's last visit to Bournville Park there are three crocuses and the lone snowdrop that bloomed after Buffy died. Each brings a tear and a smile and a fervent hope that somehow we may meet again.

ACKNOWLEDGEMENTS

First, and most importantly, I must thank Sue Murphy, Prue Neath and all the staff at the Animal Health Trust, including the charming receptionist and café staff whose friendly faces we came to enjoy seeing! So many people helped us, including Buffy's nurse, Gemma, who took such good care of her. Two other vets I recall: Lara, who performed Buffy's delicate back surgery; and Gareth, who helped design an indestructible surgical collar. The skill and dedication of all the team are second to none, as is their kindness and concern. They truly make the world a better place for the animals who go there and other visitors who benefit from their knowledge.

Cath Smith helped enormously. Buffy spent

many days at Cath's with all her pack and Buffy loved her to pieces; a true friend to Buffy and to us.

Jenny Hill, custodian of the ginger ninjas, who encouraged me to share this story.

Buffy had many friends and we thank them for their prayers and calls, encouragement and doggy presents. In Buffy's later years I visited St David's church and Buffy received healing there, so thanks to Nick the vicar for this and the prayers and small service he gave for her in the healing room.

To Phillip the librarian at Weoley Castle library, who gave helpful advice.

To all those people we met on our travels who fell in love with Buffy and may recognise themselves here, thanks to you. I hope you enjoy her story.